Photo by James DeWalt.

"For me who, during the carving process, never knew the future extent of its magic and meaning, [the poems are] a particularly extraordinary description of what goes on under the roof in ways only an observant operator who stands in the middle of the spinning creatures could know." – Scott Harrison, creator of The Carousel of Happiness

"That magical place becomes alive for the reader: music thrumming, children laughing, elders shedding time, the wounded healing, the lovers wedding themselves to the circle of life." – Christine Weeber, author of *In the Understory of Her Being* (Finishing Line Press).

OF THE CAROUSEL

POEMS BY
BURT RASHBAUM

For Lisa —
enjoy the ride!

Burt

THE POET'S PRESS
PITTSBURGH, PA

The Carousel of Happiness,
in Nederland, Colorado,
is a hand-carved carousel made by
Scott Harrison, a Vietnam veteran.
The carving took almost 26 years.
More than 100,000 riders a year
enjoy this carousel.

I am one of its operators.

I've seen it all.

OF THE CAROUSEL

a
massive
mammoth
silence
awaits
the
un
leashing
of joy
a
menagerie
of
wooden
beasts
frozen
in pose
will come
alive
creak
its 26
tons
yawn
and groan
to bear
the weight
of laughter
and tears
and pain

waiting waiting
for the first riders
to appear at
the gate

In that space
                  there is no
racism
                  no politics
no hatred
                  though t-shirts at times
so do declare

but
     he will never engage —

only joy
          and the laughter
of a
       dozen languages
the
       tears
            of distant
out of reach
ages
          and time's
unforgiving
          evolving
styles:

because who
                    won't cheer
the dancing old man

with the clown nose
who spins to the music:

                         the
operator?

The Wurlitzer is like
a beast
                    but different
from those
                    who spin and
have nicknames
                    given by
children who ride
            often.

Its roar is louder
                    than
the creaking and groaning
        of
                    the muscular machine
revolving around it —
                    louder
than arguments
                    phone calls
tantrums
            the cd-player
and the wind.

It is the only beast
                    caged
to contain its
            loudness
originally designed for
                    outdoors
now needing
mufflement

singing its 88
instruments to
the heights

protected behind
      plexi
glass
          oaken and regal
the brass horns

gleaming
like the cymbal

the snare crisp and taut
bass drum thump

makes some jump.
The Wurlitzer
        is like a

beast.

Between rides he
tells the story
of one soldier's pain

of a war the young
don't know
           of

           the loss
the searching for
          the way
to return
        to his life,
knowing
         there was a way
to return
        and finally discovering
the wood
        awaiting

         the carving of
             animals
appearing below his
          studied hand

        and reaps tears
from those who listen
            and offers
a ride on an inanimate animal

and watches

time unfold into the magic
of
    a timeless
Joy
    barely contained
within

the human form.

and she always came alone.

Looking mostly
                at the floor
no one ever talked to her
                            until
one day
            Gorilla said,
sit beside me,

so she did.

And as the massive machine
        spun
                the overpowering twenty-six tons enveloping

enwrapped raptured

                        thrum of the Wurlitzer
    would surround her with an orchestra's burst of brass

the horns blistering heights
                                the gentle piccolos
the laughing snare and hissing cymbal
admonishing the stubborn bass drum
                            throbbing with
finality,

she would hold Gorilla's hand
safe
     in his solemn embracing stare,
no questions,
          no answers,
the ride, the music, a way out
               for three and a half
minutes.

He knows something
is happening to
his body from
               within —

even before the tests
                    come back
        he knows as he

jumps up on
                 Moose, always Moose
smiling slyly
            lost in thought
                          unafraid
to bear his weight,

he's been losing weight
                        no appetite
                                   subtle pain
            needing the overwhelming

cacophony of the Wurlitzer
                          to embrace him
a cocoon of musical bombast

to be louder than the pain
                        that he knows is
eating
        his body from within.

The little bluebird on Moose's antlers said,
we were once

all trees.

He didn't remember
                    being here before.
                                    Where was here?
            Stepping up on a
plat

        form
                but no train to catch
                                here with the one who
        looks

                    so familiar
                            the animals frozen
                                        in pose
unmoving until

                    the station platform starts
        going around and around the animals and the loud loud

                                    and

the one who brought him said,
                            You loved this the last time.
                            Just like when you held me

        that day long long ago.

And he knows
           this is
his son
       this man
who sits beside him
            with a Bear
listening over

their shoulders.

Going around and around the animals and the loud loud

He knelt
      at the end of the ride by
Bear
    and asked if she'd
marry him.

The camera poised
         silent atop
the belly of the bear cub
        stationary
off the carousel

controlled by
       a friend looking down
through the
       observation window above

as the machine spun them around
and the deafening music

erased their words.

But he saw only her
       and it seemed
they were still
      while the world revolved

at a maddening pace

they were still
        as

the world returned
        in sync with
the slowing of the platform

he looked up and
        nodded
as they stopped by
        the bear cub
the tiny red light
        of the camera
lit

he knelt
and asked
        if
    she'd
marry him.

She said yes.

Sometimes he wished

he could talk. Sometimes

he hated his keyboard
                              attached
              to his wheelchair

even though it connected him.
He wished he

didn't shake so much.
But he could always talk to Panda.

No keyboard necessary no
words said
                no mis
com
      muni
ca
            tion
no mis
                    un
derstan

ding
        as the faster

he spins the calmer

he feels
going
around
no need to

work the keys
that connect him
                    to others
no need to

but the joy
                    of going
around
            air on his face
sun outside
                    shining on kids
who run
            and call each others'
names

he's taken
            out of himself
floating
            high above
the Twirling Girl
                    forever dancing
high atop
            the carousel
            out of himself
he's taken

and he's connected
                    to the animals
of wood
            buoyant with joy
taking him
as one of

their own.

He knew it was his
                 last ride, knew
it was her first,

precious cargo —
           up & down
                   up &
           down
round & round.

Hello life —
         let's go
around again

one more time.

Her laughter
         her sweet youth
recognizing him
           as her
grandfather

feeling the safety
            of
his embrace
         his tremendous
         luck
being given
        the responsibility
             of
her life

here
        on Mermaid
her sweet
                giggling
here
        better than the
music

                        knowing
her laughter as
                innate safety
in his arms

he
    hoped
            almost prayed
                        she'd remember
this one day:

spinning with
            this old man
                        to take this
memory

into the future
                her blossoming life
when he
            was long
                    long
gone.

It has to be a
        Carousel wedding
because
        there are
no aisles
        it's a circle
so they
walk
        a slow arc

to an orchestra
of cellos
        bowed by
12-year olds

and stand
before St. Bernard
who waits
        whiskey barrel
        under his chin

the sonorous strings
            call attention
to the love
        about to be sanctified

in marriage.

The air is still

as if no one
          takes even a breath.

Vows to each other
                almost whispered
to the future
            and dreams and
maybe even
                forever

as the gathered
bear witness

fill the room and
surround
            the silent
wooden menagerie
as backdrop

to their metaphor
of strength
            and endurance

through
time.

Wounded warrior
                        carrying tears
still bathed in death

needing to
leave it all behind.
Lion sighs

            just get on
I'll take it from here

                        his hands
gnarled with pain
                        knuckles
knotted and mis
                    shapen

while gentle Lion
                    a simple rose
in his mane

                    stands
unmoving
            going around
in silent strength

                    as
the wounded
                warrior

can finally
        breathe
catch a
       breath

put death
       out of his
mind

silence

the screaming
        erases
the smoke

        allows
him
      to embrace
this

simple
   spinning

as Lion slows
        as he returns
to his life

a bit less
      wounded

12

Silent sentinel
            he sits
watching:
            his strength
in no
        doubt
                as the animals
spin.

In the wild
            he would be a
terror
            hunted and feared

but the children
                come to
hug him,
            his orange striped fur
of wood

dirtied
        by ten thousand

tiny hands

and the little red
                    bird
sitting on his
            folded flank
only invites
                kisses and
caresses.

13

Serene embrace
as loving Swans
adorn the bench

gather in
mother and child
calm amid chaos

some glint of recognition
innate knowing
the music a distant

utero memory
familiar
and warm

as is her
mother's blanketed
breast

as round
they go
delirious

in sync
in rhythm
in love

with love
a delicate life
and each other.

They come by bus

with walkers
        clunking yet gliding
across

the floor
      or

in wheelchairs
         lined up
big wheels
       keep on sliding
           or

trailed by kids
        grandkids
           further descendants

matriarchs
     patriarchs
         of the family tree
              here to ride

or sometimes
        just in pairs
shuffling along
        holding hands
unaware

of exactly where
        they are
wrapped in years
        weighted with age

their lives
      frayed
and thin.

They might read
        the story
on the walls
        and think they're
back

on their carousel of 1952
or 1948 or 1961
even though
        the animals are
different

or just sit on Giraffe
        and spin
around to the sound
of the Wurlitzer's horns.

But then.
Then.

Then.
They weep
        silently at first
wiping a tear
        hoping no one
sees

them so vulnerable.

Or openly
        not caring
but not
        able
to even explain
why.

It's not happiness they feel.
It's not sadness. Open
                emotion
in a tumultuous chaos
but

the operator knows. He's
seen it. (I've seen it.)

They are experiencing
              the peeling
back of
      the fabric
        of time

lifted from their eyes
              lifted from
their shoulders
        like an old
heavy coat

revealing

the one inside
        who rode a wooden horse
in 1954 1938 1972

revealing

a self they
          long thought
sleeping or forgotten or
                    dead

suddenly
arises from within
                    and rides
and experiences
                right there
in the now

a time decades
          ago

with loved ones
          long gone

and they are a child
in the arms of
          a grandmother
born in the 19th

century. They are
                both old
and young.

Time is revealed
                as fabric
that can be peeled back

a glimpse
          back
back
          back to
their beginnings.

And as the ride
                slows
the fabric
                returns
as it must
                to where it
belongs

as they step off the platform
wiping their

mysterious tears.

15

Kids
in coned hats

young parents
unsure of their new
role

      balloons
             festoon
Rabbit's ears
         Ostrich's neck
as one renegade
        untethered
     from any child's wrist
                lazes up —
       ward to bob on
the ceiling.

A princess's glistening shoes.
A face painted to mirror Cheetah.
A wizard. A pirate. An old hippie Grandpa.

The sugar buzz
        makes everything
     go
faster. Only running
         makes sense. The
only sound
      that drowns out
the
Wurlitzer:

the chaos the glee the
                                birthday mania the
tantrums the
                    kinetic chorus the
stomping the
                          screaming the

shattering burst balloon falling

from far above their heads.

16

In between
        rides
there's
          doo wop
     a bop
bop
         shoo wop
snapping fingers

       to songs
of a distant
       rock n roll
America as
      all heads unconsciously

bob and weave
        taken to
faraway proms
         sock hops
runaround sue
       and a wish sandwich
and

The Shirelles. Until

the Wurlitzer
        brings everyone back
to the now
      and the slow spin
that slowly picks

up speed
            with echoes of ooh wa ooh wa
cool cool kitty

dancing
in their
heads.

17

Those who lack

limbs
chromosomes memory
peace love family
friends a home
a bed
a good nights

sleep
and those

who have
darkness
carved

into their hearts
                        by loss
disease
            murder
war
        pain
                nightmares

know
            the sound
means you will
                        be held
tightly
in its massive noise

you will
        find your animal

who will take the
        weight

                as
the lacking

lessens the
darkness

                recedes

hypnotized into
slumber.

18

The first life lesson
                    arrives unexpected
        unasked for
                    and unknown
to these tiny new
humans:

why does the ride
                    have to
            end?

They cannot even
                    ask the question
being pre-speech
                    beings
living on
        pure
                sensory
                    input
                            integration
                    digestion
and
overload

but they know
to react
            in horror
when the Wurlitzer
stops
        when they're being

taken away
when they point

and scream
            a kind of crying panicked pleading
a desperation
            a sudden void
where there
            had been such
joy.

Why does the ride have to end?
Why do we have to get off?
Why does the music stop?

False answers offer
                  distraction
from the sudden

subtraction:
        we have to make room for others to ride
        or time for donuts pizza the park the party
        Grandma's house to see Santa or the parade
        or because they're closing see the operator's
        sweeping the animals will soon be sleeping

but none of these
        answers
have any
            effect
there is

only
the absence now
that must

be filled
            again

a space where
                        there had been
such a something
                        so unknown til now
so needed

and the cries and tears
                        the thrashing and
        pounding on shoulders

fighting the stroller
                or the backpack

trying to get the message
across
        begging for some answer
        to a question barely born in

one so young:

why does the ride have to end?

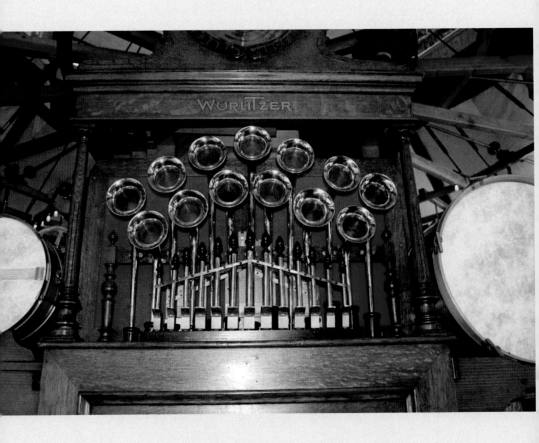

There's no arc here
             it's a circle
a huge lumbering
             creaking
thumping
        thunking
             whining
singing
        twenty-six ton dream

some old soldier's hallucination
                       drowned out
by an ancient music machine
                       drowned out
by forgotten wishes and
                   prayers and
tears, by the tension of
                   everlasting
love

and the creaking
             of wood
and old

bones

and new life.

                                        Lights out
                              all is dark
                      but for the
              redbluegreen
        lights
      along
the floor
like some
forgotten
 constellation
 the animals
 a literal
  suspended animation
   silent like a sleeping
    giant
      that still might
       groan in sleep
       so a creak
         might
            split the night
             tho the engine
                        is off. No
                         music. An occasional
                              wind.

Lights out
       all is dark
            but for the
                redbluegreen
                      lights
                    along
                        the floor
                      like some
                      forgotten
                  constellation
                  the animals
                    a literal
            suspended animation
            silent like a sleeping
                    giant
              that still might
              groan in sleep
              so a creak
              might
        split the night
       tho the engine
    is off. No
  music. An occasional
wind.

ABOUT THE AUTHOR

Born in 1953 and a native of Brooklyn, New York, Burt Rashbaum has published poetry and fiction in various literary journals and anthologies over the past three decades, most recently in *Contemporary Literary Horizons* (Bucharest) and through their chapbook series a book of poems, *Blue Pedals.* His books include the novels *The Ones That I Know* and *Tears for My Mother;* a collection of short fiction, *Becoming An American;* and one of non-fiction, *A Century of Love.* He lives in Colorado, and is one of five operators of the Carousel of Happiness in Nederland.

ACKNOWLEDGMENTS

Many thanks to the following poets who gave me excellent criticism on some (or all) of these poems and whose encouragement kept me going: Ilene Bauer, William Henry, Rattan Helgeson, Scott Harrison, Christine Weeber, John Haworth, John Callahan, and Sharon Ferguson.

ABOUT THIS BOOK

The body text of this book is Capital Serif Medium, designed by Emil & Erik Bertell and Teo Tuominen, published by Fenotype. Headlines and titles are set in Publica Slab, a font family designed by Marcus Sterz and published by FaceType. Main titles and numerals are set in Algerian, a decorative font that dates to 1907, issued by British typefounders Stephenson, Blake & Company.

Photographs of the Carousel of Happiness are by Bri Lynn Rashbaum, including the digitally-posterized image on the cover. The author portrait is by James DeWalt, used with permission.

Made in the USA
Monee, IL
10 July 2021

72909636R00045

Burt Rashbaum is one of five operators at The Carousel of Happiness, a re-imagining of a 1910 carousel with animals hand-carved by Scott Harrison, a Vietnam veteran who used his decades of carving to heal himself from the horrors of war. With ridership approaching one million, Rashbaum has had the opportunity to see a wide spectrum of life, and how riders react to the beauty of the carousel.

Rashbaum knew he could only relate his observations in the one genre that can explain the unexplainable: poetry. With a fiction-writer's eye and a poet's sensibility, he crafted these 21 poems as one sequence to reflect the beauty and wonder of The Carousel, the healing that occurs there, the life lessons, the love and indescribable joy that, as one poem states, is "barely contained within the human form."

Some poems are in the shape of the carousel; others evoke its movement, the kinetic energy of the place and the enveloping bombast of the 1913 Wurlitzer band organ that plays while the carousel spins. While the words whirl like a rider on the carousel, when they are read aloud they tell stories.

Open this book and enter The Carousel of Happiness, become a rider and experience what countless thousands from the world over have shared. Today you don't even need a ticket. All you need you hold in your hands, the poems *Of the Carousel*.

ISBN 9780922558971

90000

9 780922 558971